Help Me Say Goodbye

Activities for Helping Kids Cope
When a Special Person Dies

by Janis Silverman

Fairview Press

Minneapolis

Published by Fairview Press, 2450 Riverside Avenue, Minneapolis, MN 55454.

First Printing: January 1999

Printed in the United States of America
05 04 03 02 01   8 7 6 5 4 3

Cover and interior illustrations: *Cover Design by Laurie Duren*

For a free current catalog of Fairview Press titles, call toll-free 1-800-544-8207, or visit our web site at www.fairviewpress.org.

Preface

It is very hard to say goodbye to someone you care about. I recently had to say goodbye to my mother when she died. Her long illness and her death taught me so much about myself and about life itself. The wonderful professionals and volunteers at Woodside Hospice House in Pinellas Park, Florida, helped me through this difficult time.

Help Me Say Goodbye is a workbook for families with young children who are planning to visit a friend or family member who is dying. It walks children through a visit with a terminally ill loved one, helping them think about what they can say and do and how to deal with their feelings. *Help Me Say Goodbye* helps children and their parents cope with these circumstances in a positive way.

The book also helps children cope with the death of their loved one and find healthy ways to remember that special friend or relative. Ultimately, *Help Me Say Goodbye* can help children and their parents work through their grief in meaningful ways. As children work through their grief, they will learn about themselves and about life. They will grow from this experience, which takes them along the path from pain to accepting loving memories. Children and families may use all or part of this workbook to draw or write their feelings. They may want to keep their workbook as a lasting memory of a friend or relative who has died.

Thank you to my husband, Richard, for all of his love, support, and creative ideas.

A Note about Professional Use

This book can be used by teachers, school counselors, and children's grief counselors as part of a class or therapy situation. The children's pictures or writings will be a springboard for discussions. They will also serve as a supplement to therapy sessions.

Dedication

This book is dedicated to the memory of my mother, Florence Klein. She lives on in my heart and in the pages of this book. May this book reach out to the many children and their families who have also had to say "goodbye" to someone they love.

Some things, like sand and sea shells, don't change, but people change.

Is there someone you love who has changed?

Has this special someone been sick or hurt?

Draw your special someone.

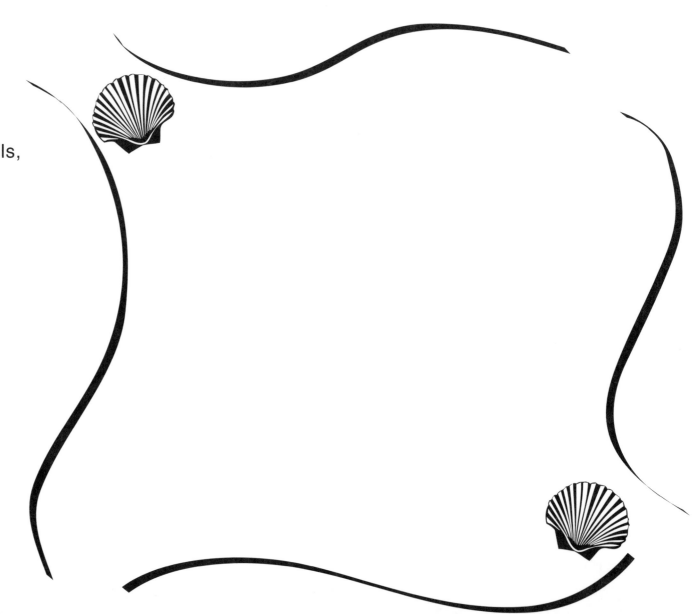

What does your special person like to do?
Write or draw some of the things your special person likes to do.

Circle the things on this page that your friend or relative can still do.

When you visit your friend or relative, what can you bring?
Draw or write about your ideas.

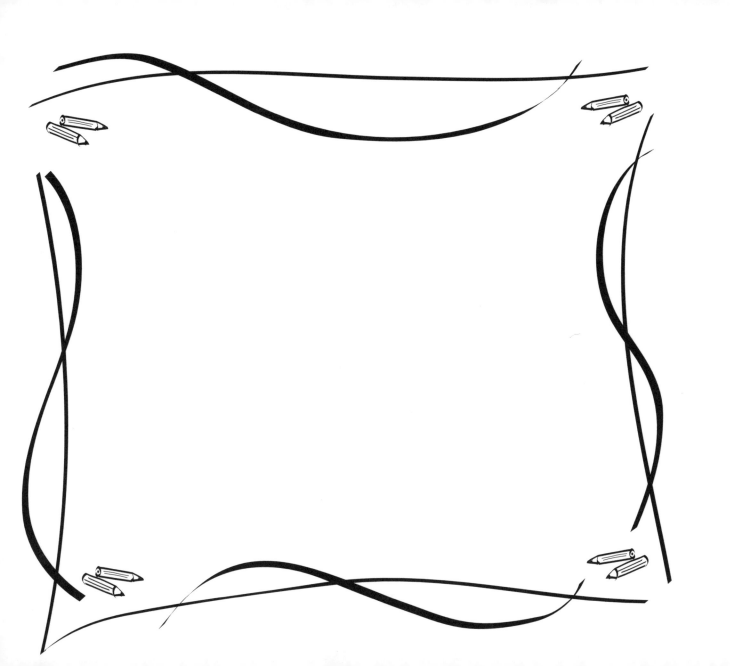

Some people get better after being sick. But some don't.

It is important for you to say goodbye to your special someone before he or she dies.

Draw or write about your feelings. Act them out or talk about them with an adult.

When your special someone is dying, what can you do to show how much he or she means to you? Draw or write your ideas.

Death is forever. After you die, you do not breathe, talk, see, hear, taste, smell, or feel anything ever again. When your special someone dies, there will be no more pain. He or she will be very still and quiet.

Draw or write about the things you remember that are no longer alive.

If you could bring something to the funeral
for your special person, what would it be?

Draw or write your suggestions.

A memory table can be a beautiful thing at a funeral service.
If you can't be at the funeral, this is still a good idea to do at home.
What would you put on your special someone's memory table?
Draw or write your thoughts.

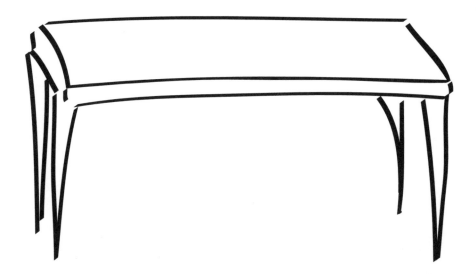

Draw a picture or write a letter to the special person who has died.
Show and explain what you will always remember about him or her.

It hurts when someone you love dies. You may feel mixed up, scared, angry, or sad. It's okay to have these feelings. This is called "grieving."

Draw or write what you are feeling when you are grieving.

When people grieve, they sometimes feel angry.
Some people yell when they are angry. Others exercise or play hard.
Draw or write what you can do when you feel angry.

Circle the things that won't hurt anyone else.
Talk with an adult about good things you can do when you are angry.

When you are grieving, you often feel sad.
Draw or write what you can do with your sad feelings.

Circle the safe choices you have drawn. Talk with a grown-up about your feelings.

Sometimes, when a special person dies, we feel like it is our fault.
We think this person died because of something we did or didn't do.

Death is not something that you can control.
It is not your fault that your special person died.

Draw about some of the things that you cannot control.

When you are grieving, other people may not know what to say.
They know that you are mixed up, scared, angry, or sad. They want to make you feel better.

It is a good idea to tell others what you need.

Draw or write about the people you can talk to about your feelings.
Remember, they are there when you need them.

When you are grieving, you may feel all alone.
It seems like your family and friends are treating you differently.

Your family and friends are grieving, too.
This means they feel mixed up, scared, angry, and sad—just like you.

Draw or write about what you can do to help others
when they are grieving.

You can't change what has happened. But you can think of better times ahead of you.
Hoping and wishing for things to get better for you and your family can help.
Draw or write about your wishes.

Here are some helpful suggestions for you:

- Say goodbye at the wake or funeral.
- Hold hands with your family at the funeral.
- Write your feelings and thoughts in a journal or diary.
- Play or be with a close friend.
- Draw pictures for or write letters to the friend or relative who has died. Keep them in a special place.
- Talk to your friend or relative as if he or she were there. Talk out your problems.
- Recall memories of your special someone.
- Play with toys and gifts given to you by the person who has died.
- Pray at church or synagogue or at home.
- Plant flowers on your friend or relative's grave. If your friend or relative was cremated, you could put flowers where the ashes are kept or buried.
- Talk to adult relatives or a counselor when you need to.
- Do some of the jobs or special things your friend or relative used to do. For example, plant a garden like he or she used to.
- Be close to your family.

- Follow in your special someone's footsteps. For example, if he or she helped the homeless, maybe you could help, also.
- Cry when you need to.
- Watch family movies.
- Look at pictures of past good times.
- Make new friends.
- Sit in your special someone's favorite chair or place.
- Go somewhere quiet to be alone and to think when you need to.
- Buy a helium balloon. Take it with you to a park or a pretty place. Let go of your sad feelings as you let go of the balloon. Watch it float away with your sad feelings.

Ideas for young children:

- Use a toy phone to talk about what happened.
- Act out what happened or how you feel with puppets or dolls.
- Draw or paint to show how you feel.
- Use clay to show your thoughts. Pound it hard if you are angry.

As time goes on and you wish to share your feelings, you can make a "feelings book." Include some things that make you feel safe and loved. Put the date on each page to show how your feelings change as time goes on.

It is good to remember your friend or relative after he or she has died.

Remembering is a way to honor your special person. It will make you feel closer to him or her. This is very important when you are grieving.

Draw or write about a special time you had with your special someone.

When a loved one dies, birthdays, holidays, and other special days can be very hard.
You might feel mixed up, scared, angry, and sad all over again.

On these days, you may want to plant a tree or
do something in memory of your special someone.
Draw or write your ideas.

You may wish to make a memory book with help from your family.

Pages may include: "My most special memory," "A letter to my special person on her birthday," or "A sad day is when I miss my special person."

Start here with your first page.

Keep something that belonged to your special person so you can touch it and look at it and remember.

Write or draw the things you have kept that belonged to your special person. Think about why these things are important to you.

Do you have a good box to keep memories in?

You could put photos and objects from your special someone in this box and look at them anytime you'd like.

Draw or write about what you might collect to put in your memory box.

What did you learn from your friend or relative? Draw or write your ideas.

Draw or write about all the quiet and peaceful
ways you can think about your special person.

Circle the ways you like best.

Death and grief teach us a lot about ourselves and about life.
Draw or write about what you have learned.

You have likely changed a lot since your special person died. Think about new things you'd like to try. Draw or write about how you are growing and changing.

Your special someone would want you to love others and to feel loved. Draw or write ways that you can share your love with others every day.